Plans

WAVE BOOKS . SEATTLE AND NEW YORK

RENEE GLADMAN

ences

Published by Wave Books

www.wavepoetry.com

Copyright © 2022 by Renee Gladman

Wave Books titles are distributed to the trade by

Consortium Book Sales and Distribution

Phone: 800-283-3572 / SAN 631-760X

Library of Congress Cataloging-in-Publication Data

Names: Gladman, Renee, artist.

Title: Plans for sentences / Renee Gladman.

Description: First edition. | Seattle : Wave Books, [2022] | Includes index.

Identifiers: LCCN 2021043221 | ISBN 9781950268597 (hardcover) | ISBN 9781950268580 (paperback)

Subjects: LCSH: Gladman, Renee—Themes, motives. | Pen drawing, American—Themes, motives.

Classification: LCC NC139.G525 A4 2022 | DDC 741.973—dc23/eng/20211004

LC record available at https://lccn.loc.gov/2021043221

Designed by Crisis

Printed in Canada

9 8 7 6 5 4 3 2 1

First Edition

Wave Books 100

These sentences—they—will begin having already been sentences somewhere else, and this will mark their afterlife, and this will be their debut

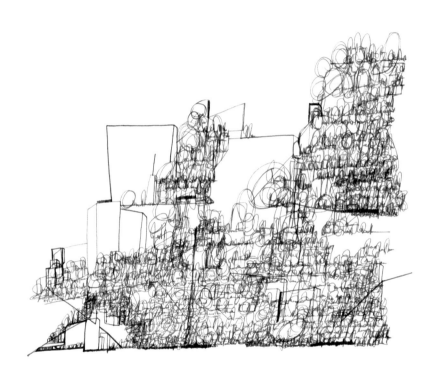

FIG. 1

These sentences will ache a massive threading of forms and will not know knowing

These will emerge from grain: they will out and open. They will over and back and open. They will edge and cross and grain

These sentences will blacken the substrate; they will go the furthest and speak the loudest in a blurred cartography. They will rise and will blacken the plain and will hold

FIG. 2

These sentences will flood the plain in a repetition of walls and living; they will bend through scaffolds and flatten as they rise and be a floor for sky

These sentences will grow the field against the substrate in a theory of hills and they will spire

They will have the one thing leaning and the other thing sloping and will divide the plain just below the densest language and will launch the language of the grain

Plans for Sentences — DB
April 2016

FIG. 3

These sentences will breathe not-breathing, will flow and blacken in the gathering

These sentences will shoal in their linearity; they will march to void and march to blacken. They will edge and thicken and double the horizon. They will blacken

These sentences will void at the plain four times, wash out the ground twice, stutter twice, elongate; they will prolong the horizon

FIG. 4

These sentences will flute and fold where the chapter crusts with questions

These will grain into a geometry of support, the history of something burrowing

These flutes will barge the void; they will silo and gather in horns draping and will take your place of speaking

They will erupt from the surface in an alternative mode of pointing and will stand variously and voidly under impulses to curve and flute; they will curve and flute without history

FIG. 5

These sentences will shade the block; they will form the substrate and shade. They will find their peaks and flutter in the corner. They will shade and flutter

These will climb the substrate: they will roll. They will roll and go quiet. They will roll, a line burning into the surface. They will over backward and will over the start and over the interruption; they will roll and square the void

These sentences will strain the curve against the graining, the diagonal against the curve, and will burn equidistant to what unfolds. They will form a scaffold of ascending and descending clauses and will know space

They will not know space

FIG. 6

These sentences will be housed among paragraphs that roll and grain; they will move vertically toward the sky, will grain, will void, amassing tiny statements

These will crust a scaffold, will chapter the site as it striates, and will write the unwritten without pause. They will encumber to void

These sentences will cover the horizon from end to end as a kind of castellation of grains and threads and portals; these portals will constitute the loop inside the map and will give the map levity

FIG. 7

These sentences will balance the question of movement against that of enclosure, will slant the rise against the cleave, and will add a portal to what you've been saying. They will out and cleave

These sentences will enact a small striation of fields, a thinning of surfaces

These sentences will move through other sentences in some accord of gravity and rotation; they will detour at the escapements then tunnel out to void

These sentences will have erupted from the plain, among the ruins of several burnt-out bunkers, your silo farm, and they will grain from the earth, each with a bending horizon and one vector pointing to space. They will cluster and contort

These will have gone up, a thin line, and bent, just going right and bending then reaching up: growing something, will grow a question an aside, an aside to the question, some stutter, and a period at the top

FIG. 8

These sentences will have moved vertically up the wall and made the floor the grain and made the grain a kind of seismic modulate unfolding

These sentences will open the chapter on the electromagnetic and will be the reeling measure, the leaning, narrowing measure that detects the underground

These sentences will thin the plain and scratch the void then cluster into undergrounds, a thinning of undergrounds; they will edge the void and blacken where they house

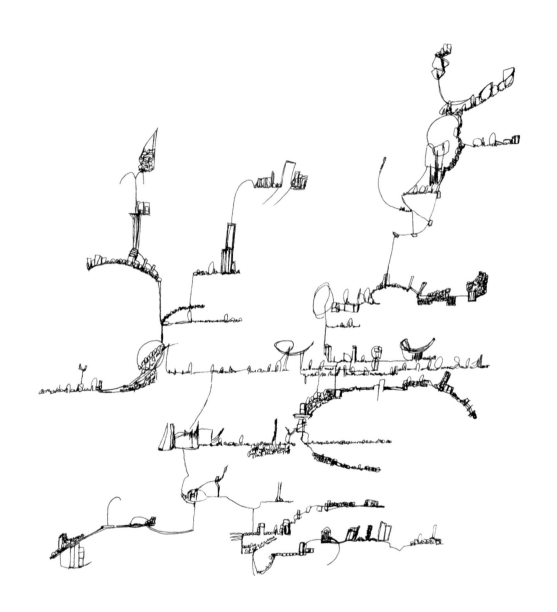

FIG. 9

These sentences will constellate the gears that alter your movements on weather; they will foment tiny gears of speech, clicking, turning, moating, and will be like wind blowing thought back onto itself, behind itself so that thought moves by leaning forward

These sentences will have performed the dreams of sentences upon arrival

These moats will separate objects from subjects and preserve silence

They will set the world of the text in motion, diverting at the escapement, turning to void, and will make small bodies of sayings that will click and moat

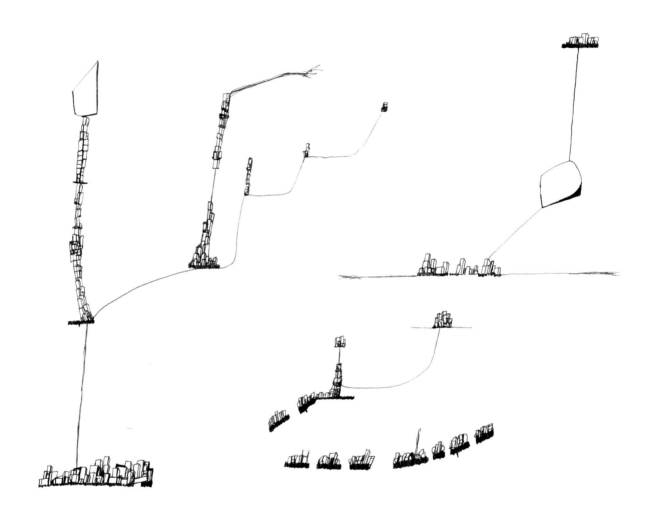

FIG. 10

These places will operate inside a thinning that brushes against the void; they will up and over and grain. They will slow and curve; they will blacken and sway in extended durations, fields of tiny neighboring enclosures

They will spire threaded towers, and behind them hives will rise belonging to language, but not these sentences of any language and not this language in particular

These sentences will gather all the pauses into a flowing assembly, into a speech that is only the comma, and will hold time as it distills and blackens in equation

FIG. 11

These sentences will dream in a thinning-leaning across the substrate; they will loop the unknown and unfinish it

These sentences will tend the slow cleaving of the field; they will over and up, they will grain and cluster, they will ripple at the edge. They will void

These sentences will seam the thinning

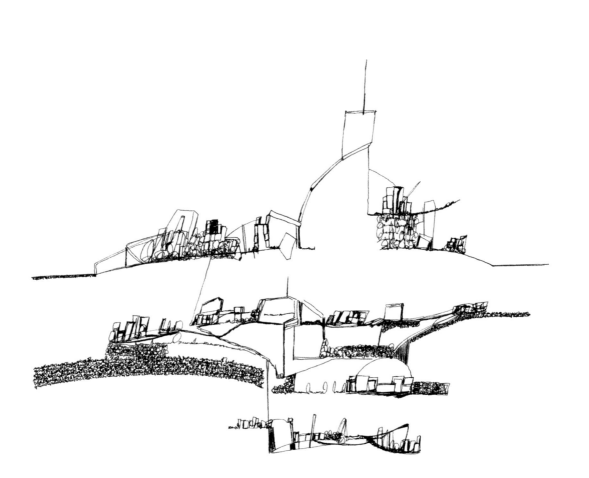

FIG. 12

These will set something at the back of something and make it larger; what is smallest will be at the forefront but also below. These will bend, will contort. They will grain

These sentences will void, giving the filament the greater voice, the one straining ladder, the cluster falling into the open; there will be gasps and graining here and a rolling out and back that ripples the paragraph

These sentences will dome the thought; they will make complex gestures and grain on a curve. They will set memories in overlapping modes of slope and cover, making hollows

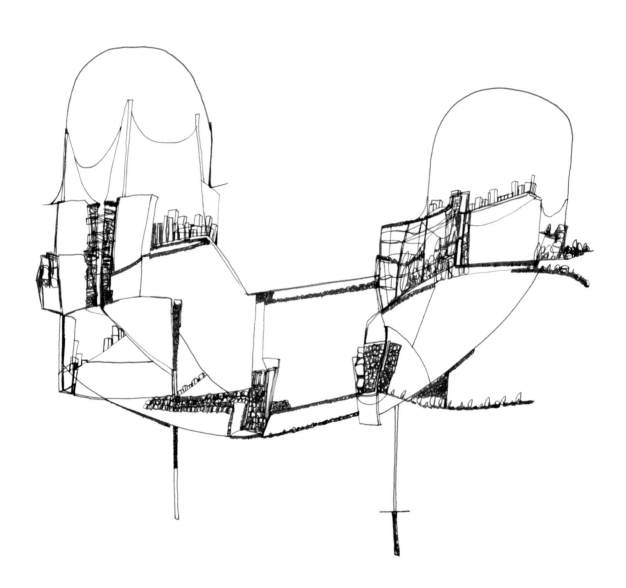

FIG. 13

These sentences will canopy, and inner sentences will flow, will slope through the space, will swing, an infectious glee growing on the columns, making tent stations and tent folds. The sound of the rectangle will out quietly, will blacken down the perimeter, push out, rise up

These sentences will double as they blacken and will make something flying be something anchored and something swooping be the inverse of something housing; and will still be a house

These sentences will awn at the ends of thought, like stiff canopies

These dwellings will form the moment the seed splits and releases the cross-section to time; they will let their walls go; they will cleave and grain. They will fold

These sentences will house the hidden beyond the curve and will thin at their saying

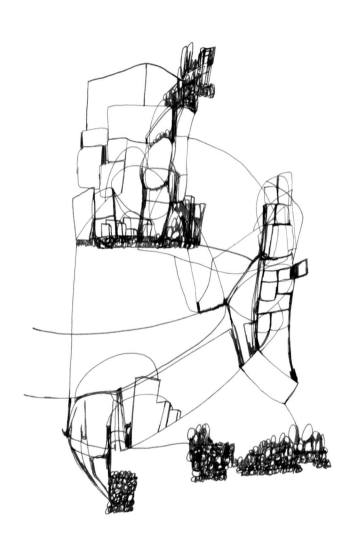

FIG. 14

These sentences will electrify the plain with black gathering; they will be blackened and will rise and cleave, magnetically, in an intake of housing

These sentences will edge the void, will edge the plain and edge the towering structure; they will grain and blacken where they house and swoop where they fail

These will flutter and spire and go dark with grain

These sentences will be half of something loving and half of something gone

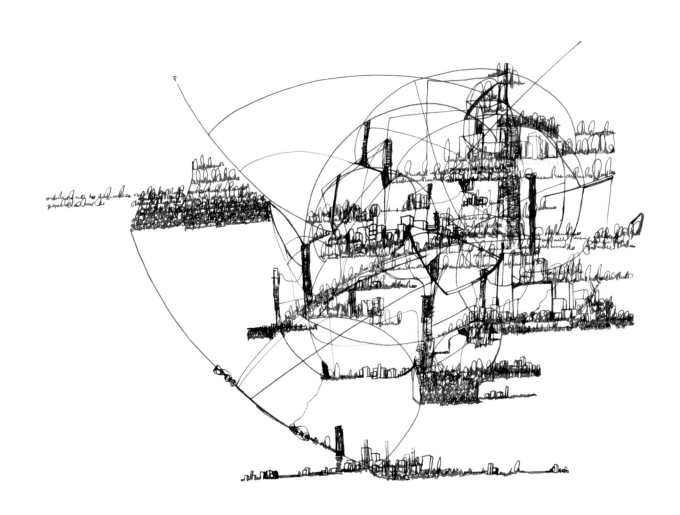

FIG. 15

These electricities will not fail in this orchestration

These electricities will fail and spire in paragraphs of self-intersection; they will spire. They will net and scaffold and will out quietly: a seabird alighting

These sentences will sonar the sea while the land mosses; they will blur where they blacken and will rise interiorly. They will out and reel and over with conduction; they will rise and thin and out

These sentences will open at a slope in a cartography of grain and wire; something will be said that is not exactly complete and it will curve, will up, will be a monument for this page

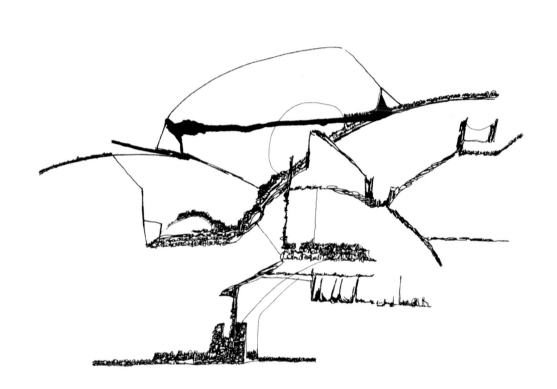

FIG. 16

These sentences will slope in their unfolding and will consent to an overlapping, to a piling on of, and will float the environment to void and will blacken it to mountain

These sentences will cluster as they break; they will grain the substrate with cover while dissolving the substrate with void. They will cluster and break, slope and cluster, slope and void, and will be a forming-devolving shape inside the chapter

They will cleave as they crust and round as they flood the plain; they will over and shade then wire and cleave; they will glow beneath the smear

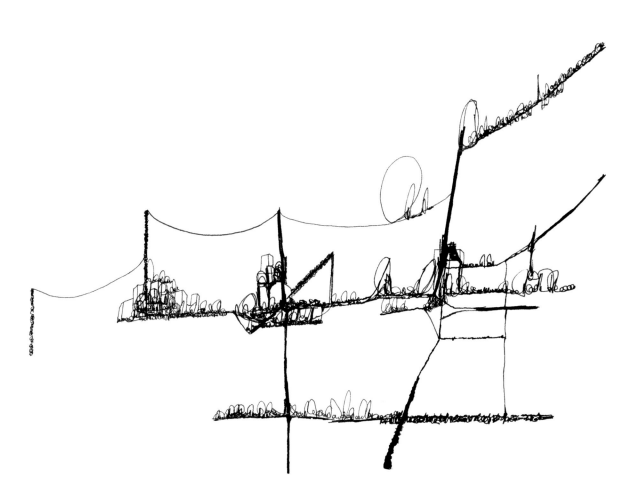

FIG. 17

These will form an assembly of poles and pour texture through the nominative

These sentences will move forward in a kind of corridor duration and will shape the stringing of something linear and climbing—calling out a gull flying over water—to something triangular and graining—calling out water in water; and they will blacken at the hinge and double the ground

These places will set the score of the ascending clause and will carry the out-and-back quietly; they will burn a line into the void, will shade harmonically the undertone

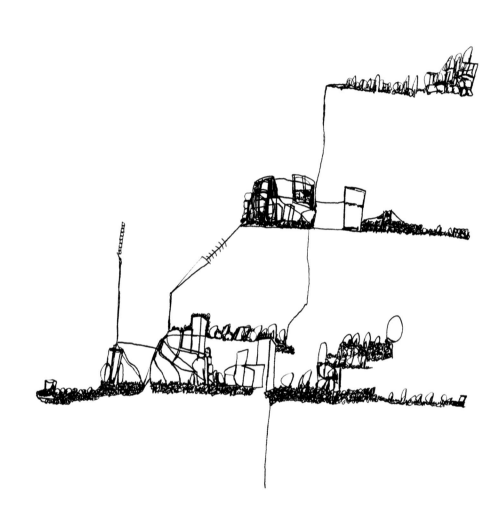

FIG. 18

These sentences will antenna the unknown and, in their phrasing, will make these wall-less floors viable for living. They will draw the poem to the silo and will lean into the sanctuary

These places will make a long dendritic break in the chapter and will open up three simultaneous currents for thought; they will grain at the edge and fail; they will spire where they thin and void

These sentences will grain along the seam, will blacken the seam, will thread through the seam three times and three times will thread its unsaying

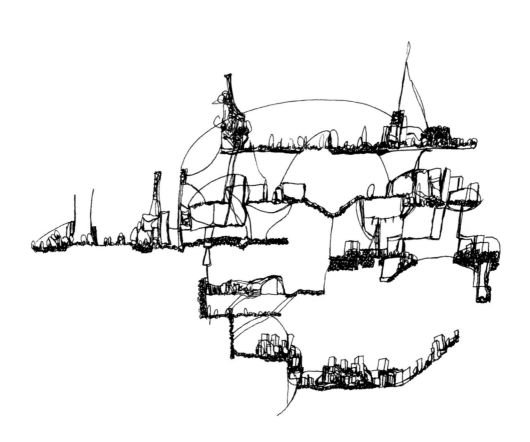

FIG. 19

This chapter will open the face of the book, revealing a series of active escapements, linking place to place. These will steady the dissolving map, be an intricacy of dome, be a slope cut along an edge

These places will keep the apex and the wire at opposite ends of trying and will round the phrase into tiny enclosures

These will cleave in tiny gasps of living, one on top of another; they will run the circle of the page and will leave the circle to the void; they will dome and out quietly

These will out and over and grain and through and around; they will shade and climb the sub-strate and spire. They will shade and cut the plain, leave a ladder

FIG. 20

These sentences will line the plain in modules for listening; they will hold and wait and lean in an absence of weather; they will be the calmative for the field

These sentences will make a tight, enclosing harmonics where the linking phrases turn and gasp in miniature and will lean in muted light

These will distill the question about the weather—"Is it fine?" "Are you fine today?" They will flute and silo

FIG. 21

These sentences will appear in a suspension of one hundred micro-substrates full of two hundred open clauses; they will bend instead of spire, will lichen and climb the retaining substrate wall

These places will dream of themselves and place images of their details in proximity to their own construction; they will arc and repeat as they wander and will be the same arc numerously

These sentences will dome their alliances and make a castellation through a succession of awns

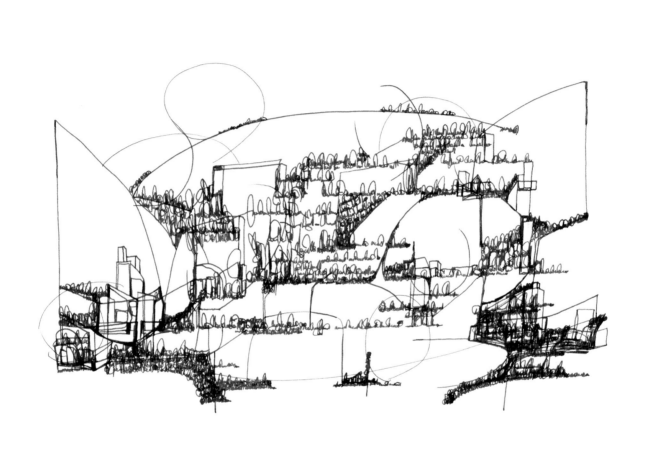

FIG. 22

These sentences will ache a not-knowing of forms and will awn where they breathe

These sentences will move around an extending gasping, a series of openings in the field; they will pour texture as an intervening and will awn in the leaves, the chapter growing dark where they gather

These places will emerge out of a thinning that lifts the chapter up and loops the plain, that loops the void, making monuments

These sentences will grow grasses as the chapter ends and these grasses will signal the plain but also cut the substrate. Yet, the structure will hold. These will be the gaps

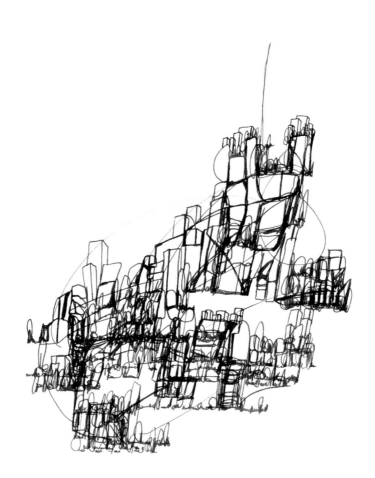

FIG. 23

They will out quietly in a thin single line of fanning, they will turn, they will counter; they will turn and land and lift off and turn within the meditation, and will blacken gasps into the page

These places will inscribe their own topography: make their shape with their shape. And will sonar inside the void

These sentences will wind tightly around who we are and how we live and will grow habitations as they wonder; they will cleave from the ground in enclosures of grief and will knoll

FIG. 24

These will shoal and form a chamber just outside the dream; they will assume the energy of a dispersing hive and will blight the history

These will hive; they will bellow

FIG. 25

These sentences will erase half of what they say and will blight. They will make an unraveling that will void at the edges and will be an inland going from blight to grain; they will grain

These places will know a cleave from a cluster and will organize what we've said by density; the gathering will skew the language order, these sentences, the wind that will have moved them

These places will be built upon a geometry embedded in the cluster that is a new picture of figuration: a blackening of the figure and a blackening of the ground

FIG. 26

These places will foment

They will send out fraying signals, will lean away from the hull and into the wing

They will be made of wind and will gasp, will allow gasps to become walls then will bellow and fray

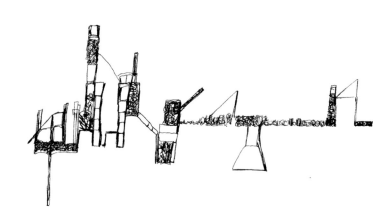

FIG. 27

These places will spell out a proof for the thinning of surfaces in their own unrelated thinning; they will grain

They will build upon a notion of the half-silo, the floorless outdoors

These sentences will make a small equation against three thin lines cutting at the diagonal and will go quiet at the edge

FIG. 28

These places will erupt along the line between worlds, visible and invisible; they will cluster along the substrate, magnetically, and will be a moving field

These will be sentences upon which is reflected something unseen seeing. They will foment where they empty, go quiet where they flood, be a staggering response to something missing, be a hull, a curve

They will sonar the erased

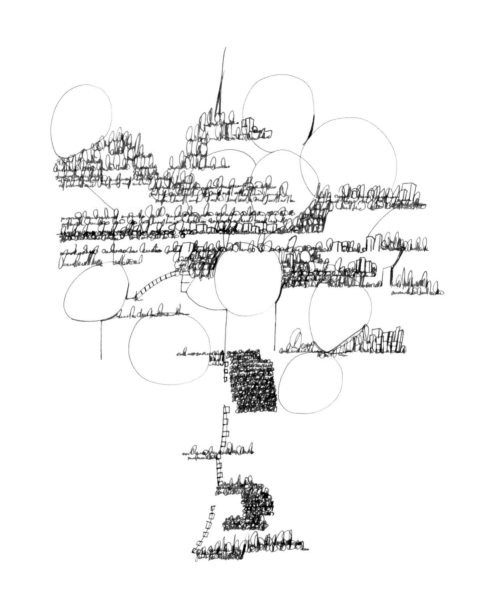

FIG. 29

These sentences will funnel the plain in a bout of weather between the boundary and the front; they will rotate above and grain below. They will over and back above, will grain and blacken below. They will make an underground for your breathing, a repeating of devoted enclosure

These sentences will form a sanctuary for refusal; they will fan out, they will awn and cleave a new scaffold

These will have ended in a spire, in reach of elsewhere, the other side of bringing things in to know them; they will have wanted to preserve the gasps as tiny communities but will have been thought mostly to void, to believe upward, and will have finished at the filament

FIG. 30

These thinning structures will be blowing in high winds for as long as this chapter exists, which will be always; they will tendril in loose piles and be like portals through the substrate. They will rise as they thin

FIG. 31

These sentences will river around silence and will out and vanish

They will roll out of light into light

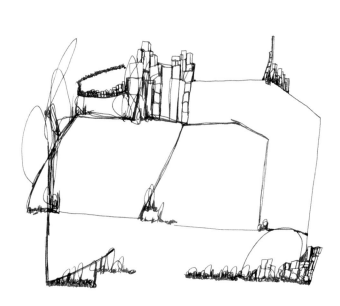

FIG. 32

These sentences will round then slope then lapse; they will void then thin then fail. They will cluster at the edge and open. They will round at the edge and void

These sentences will round and hold as they lean; they will void in their interior but will hold. They will cleave the last refrain and go quiet; they will open and blacken

FIG. 33

These sentences will awn the ethereal in formations of slow, climbing subjunctives; they will match the speed of that which has not occurred and that which is not yet known, and will show the stillness of that speed

These curved enclosures will thin the plain; they will gasp where they void, will void where they cleave

These places will gather in a succession of hollows, just edging above the grass, in effigy of the known, fraying; they will slant and hold and fray above the void, in and around the plain

FIG. 34

These sentences will be the collective wondering about change; they will grain and blacken in the wings where the paragraph breaks open and will congregate around the question: Are we fine?

These sentences will have vectors that enter where they edge and will go to hollows, will curve to void and cleave to edge; they will funnel fourteen times and void

These will slope from trying

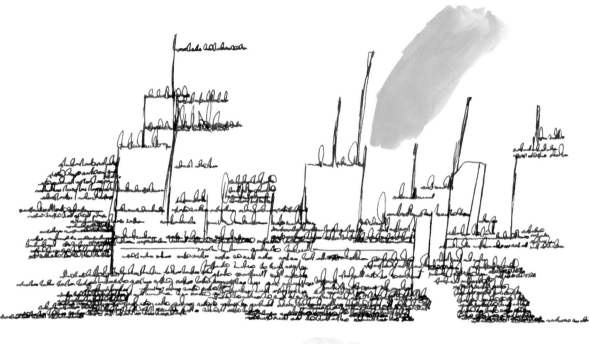

FIG. 35

These places will glow and will void and stick like wet leaves at the window, partitioning thought, condensing the gasps to grains: they will roll forward, backward, will roll and contract breathing. They will antenna the opening

These sentences will be the breathing on the other side of the paragraph; they will open and roll and roll and go quiet, backward over spent breath, graining the vapors

These sentences will arrive in a weather system; they will glow and pound the coast

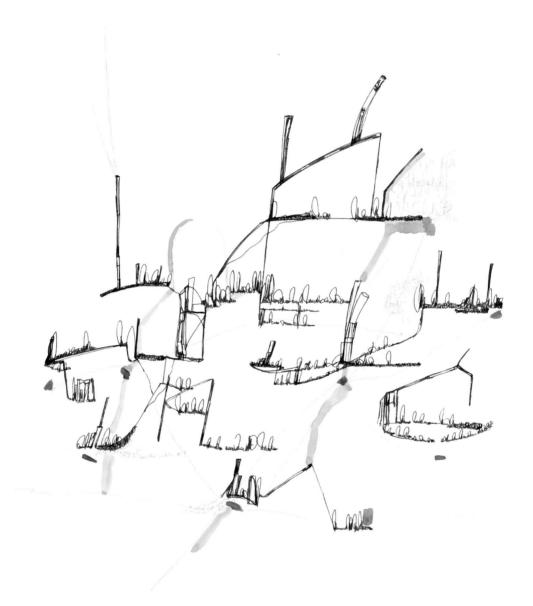

FIG. 36

These will hang in staggered formation for what you're saying and will corner and roll; they will be the glowing chapters and will show the ley lines beneath the weather report

These will name little waters that comma, that lean

These places will let evening glow through them and outline thresholds of ascendant and descendant thinking; the floors will sphere with a notable absence of walls

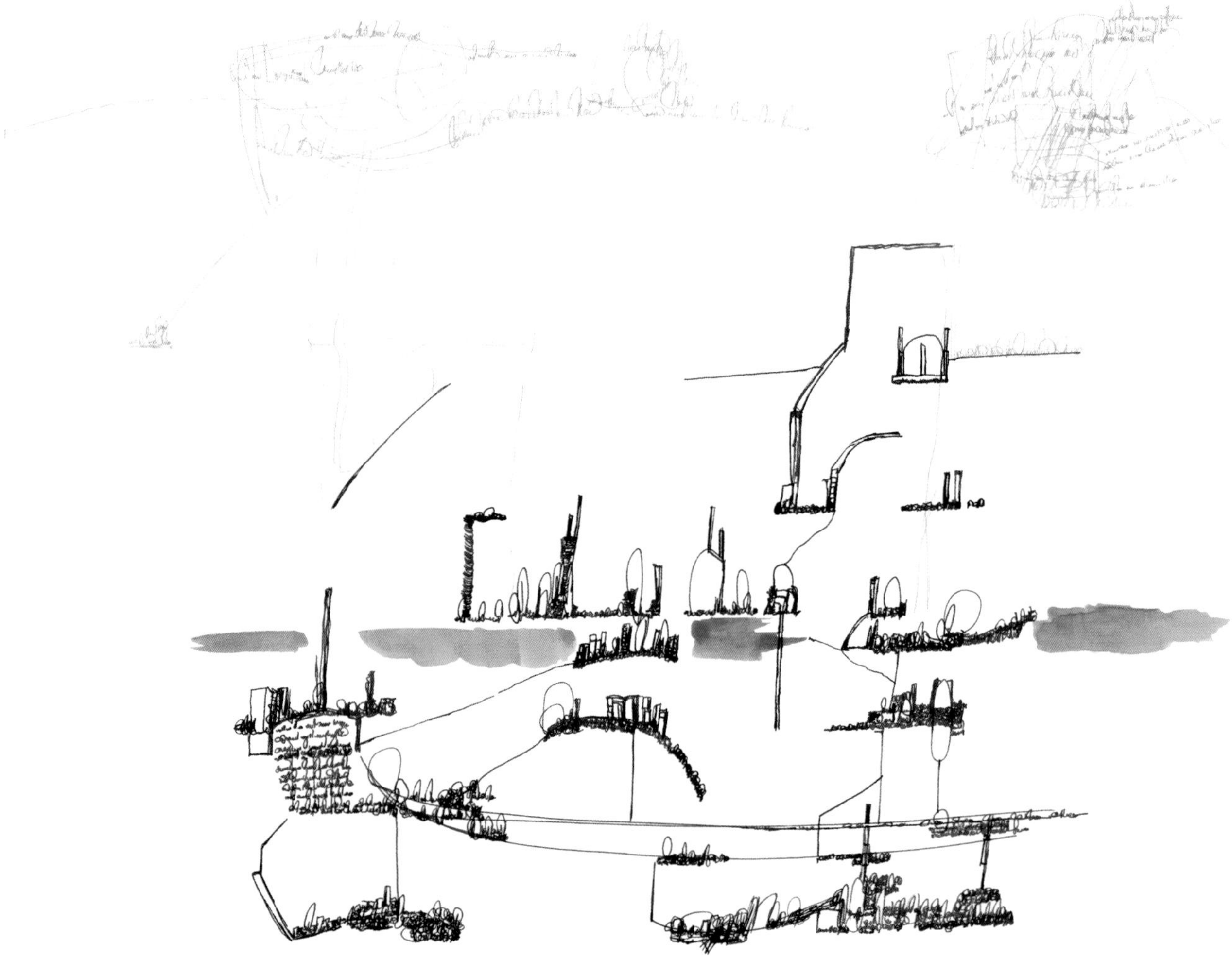

FIG. 37

These sentences will take the line of the smear without smearing and will fall below the fault of the page; they will grain and cluster independent and complete of the horizon

These places will not always be where they are and will not always remain intact and only will be measured at the points where they erase themselves and by the thrum of their evacuation

These places will tendril when everyone is sleeping and will lay down wall-less paragraphs that are legible only when unseen

These sentences will have climbed the helical field, been a scaffolding of filaments, elaborations on thinning in thinning air, airless atmosphere—all air

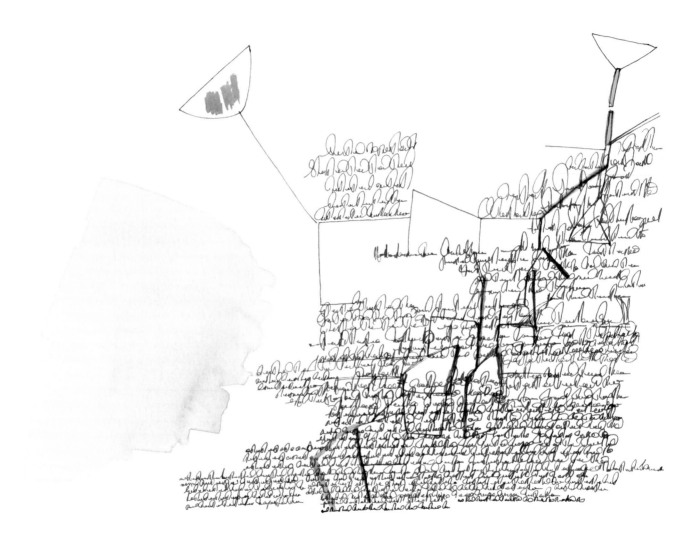

FIG. 38

This chapter will ache a massive threading and glow; it will stand at the end of all chapters and reclaim its geometries. It will weather and glow in an overlay of forms and will buckle where it cleaves

These will be sentences that climb and blacken after fog, that fog out with wanting. They will roll tightly against the substrate then will bellow

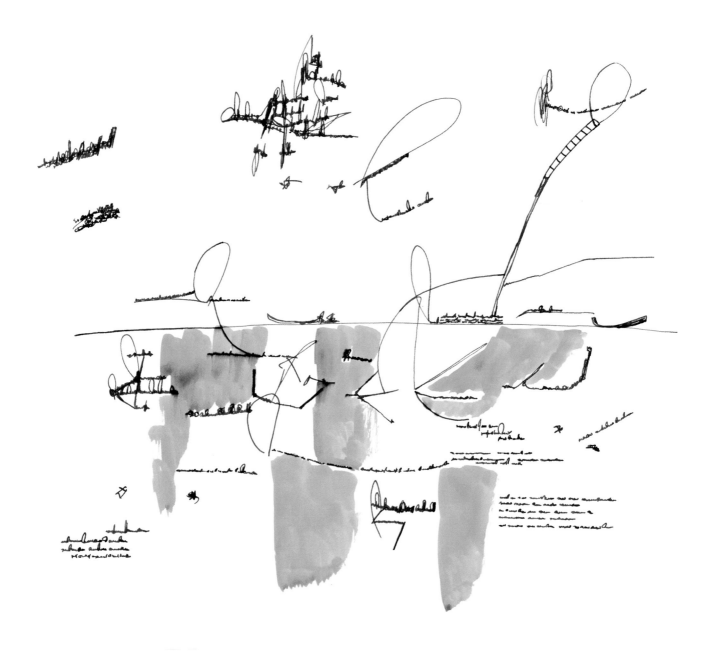

FIG. 39

These sentences will be a figuration of birds flying above a ground on fire, under fire, sentences returning

These sentences will be electrically wired half-structures that glow where they falter. Their wires will out; they will over and back and will fail where they thin and void

These sentences will glow where they blacken and be a figuration of edge to void to slope to void and will cleave as an outpost

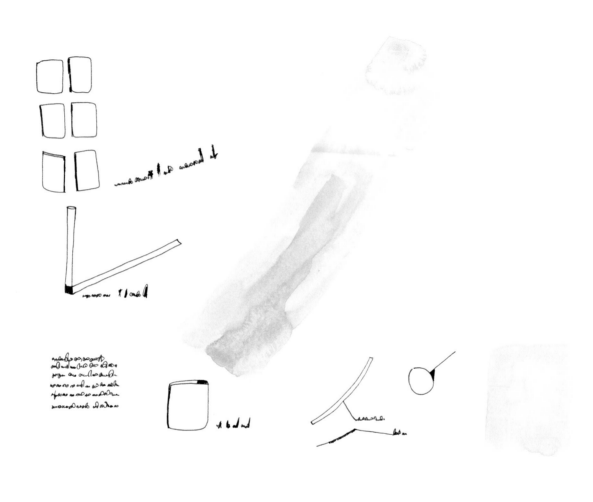

FIG. 40

This chapter will slide into your math diaphanously and will make a memoir of your space problem: the concentric to the grain upon the slope to the stacked. It will blacken with enfoldment

These sentences will form a canopy of slow-moving sites and will cluster after fog and open after quiet

They will stack and out and hinge. These sentences will hold; they will slope and edge and double. They will fail at the thinning. They will double in the center

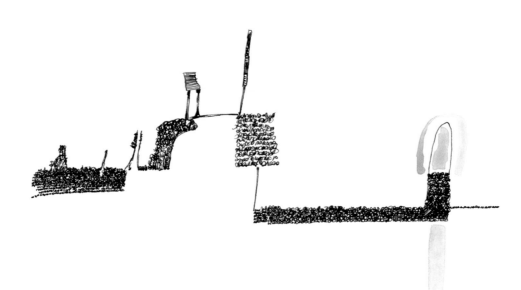

FIG. 41

These sentences will have a prop for resting at their centers, a pause in their unfolding for the subject, a bridge for wonder. They will thin where they close and will parse the luminous

They will make a system out of graining and will build on the break; they will sit, they will stand then void. They will thin then crust then glow; they will elapse. They will grain an underground, a bright hollow

This chapter will be the dark glowing fog over the substrate, the void opening to cleave; it will edge the unwritten into a shape of something wrote and will be read from graining, be a thinning

FIG. 42

These sites will be your monuments in cloud-heavy paragraphs; they will blacken and be your underground. They will curve and thin and will awn after closing; they will fail in twilight

These will exist without walls but will have domes then fog

They will be wall-less, curved enclosures for voice, clauses for loss, graining for the collective; they will open and climb and swoop diaphanously

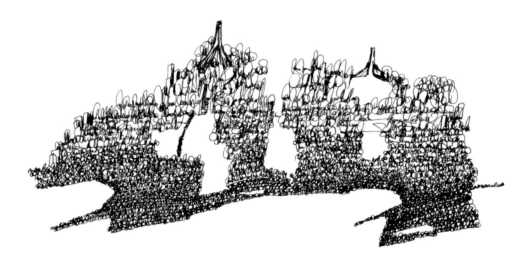

FIG. 43

These sentences will build the shoals of previous sentences into the shoals of those prior until they invert the erosion of the plain; they will umbel the afterword into a funnel and make a bridge of funnels to void

These sentences will hive and grain within an enfoldment; they will dream where they cleave and void against blight, rising out of the plain. They will spire and roll and open. They will slope and hum and filament the slow-going

These sentences will narrow in an out-and-through and leave behind a blackening that is also a map: they will tendril and grain and rise with nominative force. They will close the caption

FIG. 44

This chapter will have exploded from its interior shading and will enumerate with force, in a force of clouds

These will be events returning

These will be the sky written on and the sky extending to the ground; these will blur their borders, they will lean and darken and partition the ground from itself. These will be weather

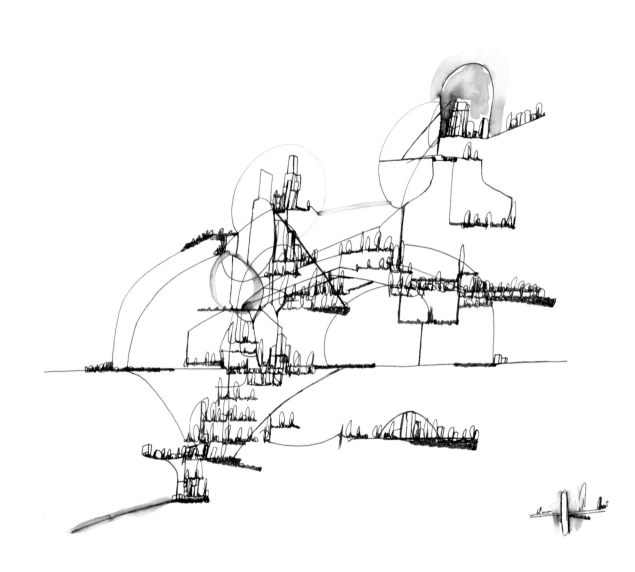

FIG. 45

These sentences will both fog and chart the rising structure. They will dome as they scroll on a slant; they will slant and tendril and make a knot of the caption

This chapter will write itself in intervals of fog and twilight; it will filament the curve and be a chronicle. It will curve and close then curve and fog and will glow where it blackens. It will grain and blacken and void

These sentences will lattice the substrate into composites of light and wire; they will fog the monument in a curving; they will fog the ground in memory. They will void the key

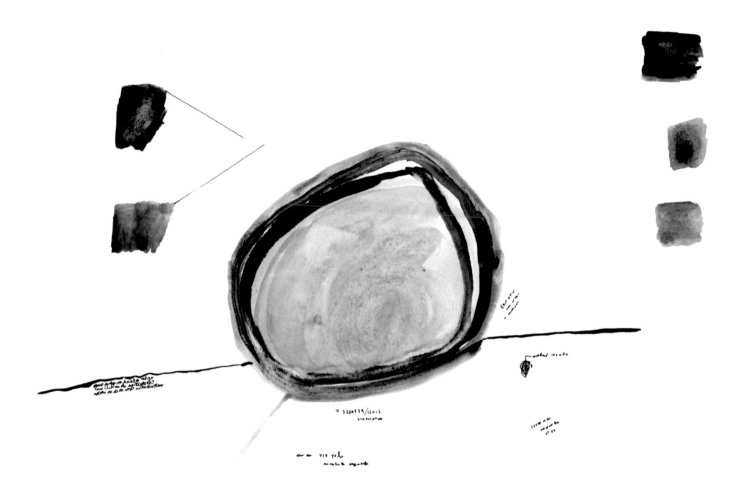

FIG. 46

These sentences will model a scale of the exhaustion of the erased

This chapter will represent a gap in the paragraph, a time between words, and will shade loudly the evacuated and be a black luminous, slow-going forward

These sentences will dream themselves into a figuration of planets and satellites, looking to set value to variables beyond the science of the plain: the feeling of the unknown beside you

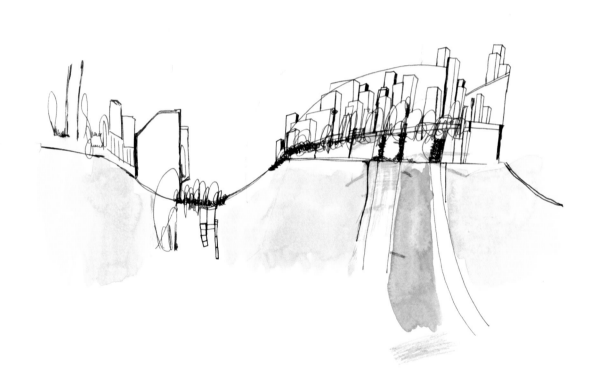

FIG. 47

These sentences will emerge as sites built haphazardly upon a fog ground and will be winded

They will have speed, and this will be what pleases, what funnels the valley to void; they will have gasps where they bridge and will figment

These places will perform gestures of welcome; they will drop where they glow and be enclosing; they will open where they fail

FIG. 48

These sentences will be places of moss

These places will emerge from something thick inside something glowing and will light upon a series of dense clauses, a paragraph for the planet

These dense woods will hold the history of where we moss and where we blacken and will be the fog void, inverted and full

FIG. 49

These sentences will drop the nominative as a translation of sticks, geometrically, and will pull the number to the letter, will pour texture on the plain and crust the chapter

This chapter will comprise 465 passages without words; and there will be a gray happening

These sentences will combine at dawn, intersecting sightlessly, and will not always say what they mean but will be breathing

FIG. 50

These paragraphs will be the boundary between wind and ground and will be woven into the thing that is writing; they will be a feeling of the thing in motion but will hang invisibly to void

These sentences will be a duration of grasses succumbing to water

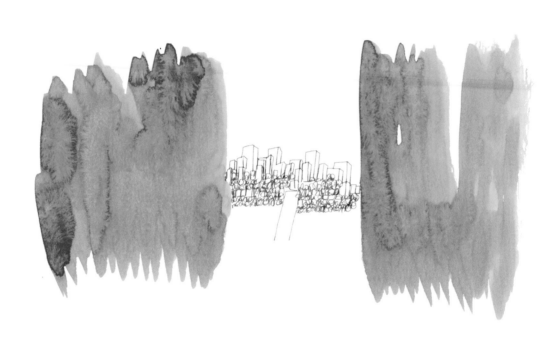

FIG. 51

These sentences will have retreated into the territory long before we arrive, so what they say will be too quiet and too cold to hear; they will sit between two impossible walls in our dream of the journey, voiding against the rectangle

These will be those tiny sentences that come at the end of some meandering thought, stuttering between conclusion and silence

This chapter will be the site of all the commas fleeing

FIG. 52

These places will open as domes in an immediate and continuous state of becoming something other: domes to spire, domes to fog, domes failing

These places will be held in the wild thinning of the afterword; they will blacken and be a scaffold. They will fold and thin and be set to motion; they will fail and thin and hollow. They will hold

These sentences will work the ground of the dreaming chapter into a commotion of waking: the ground waking inside the dream, the chapter waking inside a moving torque of hills

FIG. 53

These sentences will take place in three modes simultaneously; they will shade in the measure of the space that holds them and curve to laddering, making a lattice but only up to void. They will out where they void and return where they edge and will forget themselves

These sentences will be moments of partitioned saying, thinking separated by semicolons and math; they will field the interior stream and will reach and shade and roll quietly forward

SYSTEMATIC
TREATMENT OF
MAGNITUDE

FIG. 54

These places will tower in their seeing with fog rolling over; they will broadcast without disclosing their content. These will out and blacken; they will up in glowing speed

These sentences will have repeated while entrenching and will have glowed while rolling and will have been the systematic treatment of magnitude, being the underdoings of the colon, the em dash, the room behind the side of

This chapter will be the weather report on full blast, your opening paragraph moaning: so much light

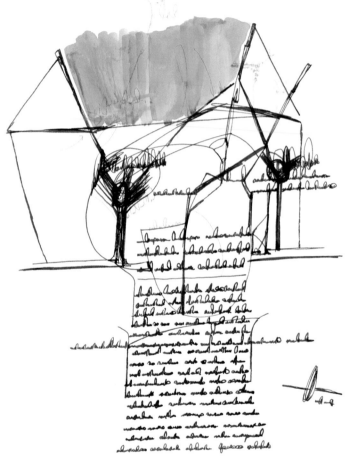

FIG. 55

These sentences will reflect many places sitting in the same place; they will rise with breathing and will fold at the apex

These places will leak their histories and will void; they will burn lines into the walls of the page and will haunt the periphery with figuration

These sentences will keep their core lit throughout the event of this writing and will attempt to grow a floor out of an introduction then build an essay under the floor and have math be the ghosts

These sentences will be on fire by the time the dream arrives and will not want the dream, will be in a state of both narrating the dream and tearing it apart; these will have speed as they burn, will fray

FIG. 56

These sentences will bring about dome stations in flickering reading light, will half-dome the dependent clause; they will curtain and time the corner glow; will strike, will curve around a graining

These sentences will gesture morning in the talking structure; they will be the blackening of the plain and the crowding of the light, be erased by light, without wind

These sentences will draw inward when they arrive at the diaphanous chapter, the how-to-build, how-to-bridge chapter, and will be a blackened scree inside the luminous hidden within a proposition of houses

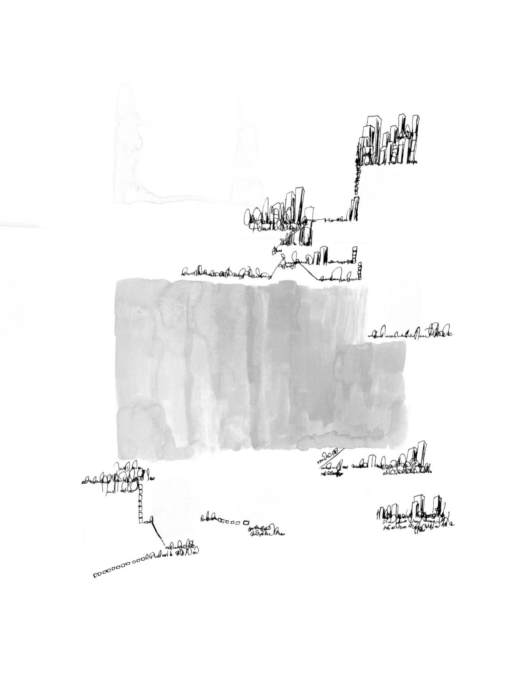

FIG. 57

These sentences will turn fog into gaps and will allow the page to become a turning; something will turn that also will out and back quietly. The outside will glow from inside, becoming a window

These sentences will signal the closing of the figurations, the soon-to-be end of planning, the growing short of breathing

These sentences will move invisibly through their not-knowing

These sentences will filament the connection between phrases; will gasp the void and comma. They will detail the thinning of structures and will be the thinning itself

These will be the inhabitable sentences

FIG. 58

This chapter will be about laughter and a doming light; there will be gasps and a set of ascending enclosures, everything moving up on a slope, curving as it rolls out

These places will write the sky, as if below every bridge, and will smear the plain with something hiding

These sentences will blacken as the waters draw near; they will scaffold around the curving. They will out and up and close; they will round and tighten and close; they will out to void

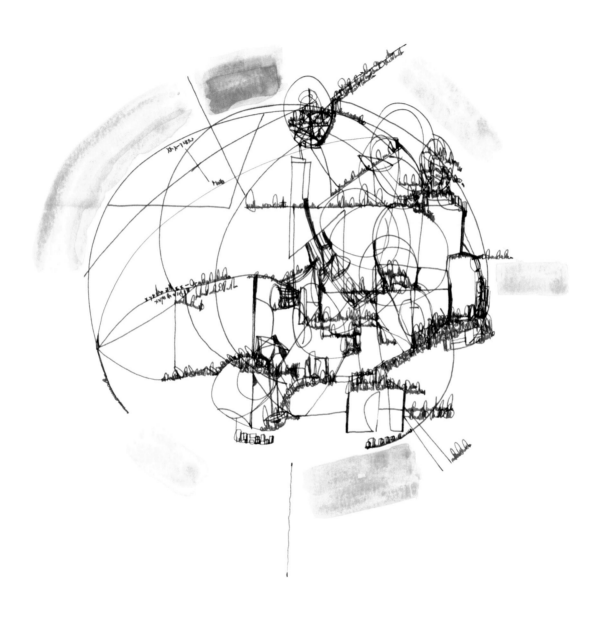

FIG. 59

These sentences will constellate the territories of the poem and will be the unraveling of the middle interior sky, too early arriving to the membranous sky, and will thin to the exterior

These equations will mark the change from a curving closing to a curving diagonal and will grain at the apex; they will void in the water and void at the filament

This chapter will self-intersect as well as any poem or weather map; it will blacken as it figures: be a thinning, be dark. And will chart a history of wander

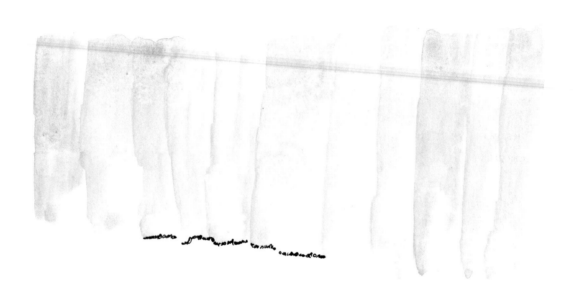

FIG. 60

These sentences will be that day of cloud cover that shelters the unwritten, that unfolds as folds of invisible material in time; they will write lightlessly. They will glow and be dark and will graze the substrate, be a presence tilting the planet: one black, twelve longitudes

These places will have wind and fog and lines pulled up from the earth in an emergence of ground; they will funnel the void in an expanse of housing. They will be wall-less

These places will be the last of it, before the beginning sets in, emerging from the plain dissolving it. They will out, they will up and flutter and through. They will out and quiet; they will blacken and open and will shelter

These sentences will have shelter

DESCRIPTIONS OF FUTURE SENTENCES, AN INDEX

These curved enclosures will thin the plain; they will gasp where they void, will void where they cleave [66]

These dense woods will hold the history of where we moss and where we blacken and will be the fog void, inverted and full [96]

These dwellings will form the moment the seed splits and releases the cross-section to time; they will let their walls go; they will cleave and grain. They will fold [26]

These electricities will fail and spire in paragraphs of self-intersection; they will spire. They will net and scaffold and will out quietly: a seabird alighting [30]

These electricities will not fail in this orchestration [30]

These equations will mark the change from a curving closing to a curving diagonal and will grain at the apex; they will void in the water and void at the filament [118]

These flutes will barge the void; they will silo and gather in horns draping and will take your place of speaking [8]

These moats will separate objects from subjects and preserve silence [18]

These paragraphs will be the boundary between wind and ground and will be woven into the thing that is writing; they will be a feeling of the thing in motion but will hang invisibly to void [100]

These places will be built upon a geometry embedded in the cluster that is a new picture of figuration: a blackening of the figure and a blackening of the ground [50]

These places will be held in the wild thinning of the afterword; they will blacken and be a scaffold. They will fold and thin and be set to motion; they will fail and thin and hollow. They will hold [104]

These places will be the last of it, before the beginning sets in, emerging from the plain dissolving it. They will out, they will up and flutter and through. They will out and quiet; they will blacken and open and will shelter [120]

These places will dream of themselves and place images of their details in proximity to their own construction; they will arc and repeat as they wander and will be the same arc numerously [42]

These places will emerge from something thick inside something glowing and will light upon a series of dense clauses, a paragraph for the planet [96]

These places will emerge out of a thinning that lifts the chapter up and loops the plain, that loops the void, making monuments [44]

These places will erupt along the line between worlds, visible and invisible; they will cluster along the substrate, magnetically, and will be a moving field [56]

These places will foment [52]

These places will gather in a succession of hollows, just edging above the grass, in effigy of the known, fraying; they will slant and hold and fray above the void, in and around the plain [66]

These places will glow and will void and stick like wet leaves at the window, partitioning thought, condensing the gasps to grains: they will roll forward, backward, will roll and contract breathing. They will antenna the opening [70]

These places will have wind and fog and lines pulled up from the earth in an emergence of ground; they will funnel the void in an expanse of housing. They will be wall-less [120]

These places will inscribe their own topography: make their shape with their shape. And will sonar inside the void [46]

These places will keep the apex and the wire at opposite ends of trying and will round the phrase into tiny enclosures [38]

These places will know a cleave from a cluster and will organize what we've said by density; the gathering will skew the language order, these sentences, the wind that will have moved them [50]

These places will leak their histories and will void; they will burn lines into the walls of the page and will haunt the periphery with figuration [110]

These places will let evening glow through them and outline thresholds of ascendant and descendant thinking; the floors will sphere with a notable absence of walls [72]

These places will make a long dendritic break in the chapter and will open up three simultaneous currents for thought; they will grain at the edge and fail; they will spire where they thin and void [36]

These places will not always be where they are and will not always remain intact and only will be measured at the points where they erase themselves and by the thrum of their evacuation [74]

These places will open as domes in an immediate and continuous state of becoming something other: domes to spire, domes to fog, domes failing [104]

These places will operate inside a thinning that brushes against the void; they will up and over and grain. They will slow and curve; they will blacken and sway in extended durations, fields of tiny neighboring enclosures [20]

These places will perform gestures of welcome; they will drop where they glow and be enclosing; they will open where they fail [94]

These places will set the score of the ascending clause and will carry the out-and-back quietly; they will burn a line into the void, will shade harmonically the undertone [34]

These places will spell out a proof for the thinning of surfaces in their own unrelated thinning; they will grain [54]

These places will tendril when everyone is sleeping and will lay down wall-less paragraphs that are legible only when unseen [74]

These places will tower in their seeing with fog rolling over; they will broadcast without disclosing their content. These will out and blacken; they will up in glowing speed [108]

These places will write the sky, as if below every bridge, and will smear the plain with something hiding [116]

These sentences will ache a massive threading of forms and will not know knowing [2]

These sentences will ache a not-knowing of forms and will awn where they breathe [44]

These sentences will antenna the unknown and, in their phrasing, will make these wall-less floors viable for living. They will draw the poem to the silo and will lean into the sanctuary [36]

These sentences will appear in a suspension of one hundred micro-substrates full of two hundred open clauses; they will bend instead of spire, will lichen and climb the retaining substrate wall [42]

These sentences will arrive in a weather system; they will glow and pound the coast [70]

These sentences will awn at the ends of thought, like stiff canopies [26]

These sentences will awn the ethereal in formations of slow, climbing subjunctives; they will match the speed of that which has not occurred and that which is not yet known, and will show the stillness of that speed [66]

These sentences will balance the question of movement against that of enclosure, will slant the rise against the cleave, and will add a portal to what you've been saying. They will out and cleave [14]

These sentences will be a duration of grasses succumbing to water [100]

These sentences will be a figuration of birds flying above a ground on fire, under fire, sentences returning [78]

These sentences will be electrically wired half-structures that glow where they falter. Their wires will out; they will over and back and will fail where they thin and void [78]

These sentences will be half of something loving and half of something gone [28]

These sentences will be housed among paragraphs that roll and grain; they will move vertically toward the sky, will grain, will void, amassing tiny statements [12]

These sentences will be moments of partitioned saying, thinking separated by semicolons and math; they will field the interior stream and will reach and shade and roll quietly forward [106]

These sentences will be on fire by the time the dream arrives and will not want the dream, will be in a state of both narrating the dream and tearing it apart; these will have speed as they burn, will fray [110]

These sentences will be places of moss [96]

These sentences will be that day of cloud cover that shelters the unwritten, that unfolds as folds of invisible material in time; they will write lightlessly. They will glow and be dark and will graze the substrate, be a presence tilting the planet: one black, twelve longitudes [120]

These sentences will be the breathing on the other side of the paragraph; they will open and roll and roll and go quiet, backward over spent breath, graining the vapors [70]

These sentences will be the collective wondering about change; they will grain and blacken in the wings where the paragraph breaks open and will congregate around the question: Are we fine? [68]

These sentences will blacken as the waters draw near; they will scaffold around the curving. They will out and up and close; they will round and tighten and close; they will out to void [116]

These sentences will blacken the substrate; they will go the furthest and speak the loudest in a blurred cartography. They will rise and will blacken the plain and will hold [2]

These sentences will both fog and chart the rising structure. They will dome as they scroll on a slant; they will slant and tendril and make a knot of the caption [90]

These sentences will breathe not-breathing, will flow and blacken in the gathering [6]

These sentences will bring about dome stations in flickering reading light, will half-dome the dependent clause; they will curtain and time the corner glow; will strike, will curve around a graining [112]

These sentences will build the shoals of previous sentences into the shoals of those prior until they invert the erosion of the plain; they will umbel the afterword into a funnel and make a bridge of funnels to void [86]

These sentences will canopy, and inner sentences will flow, will slope through the space, will swing, an infectious glee growing on the columns, making tent stations and tent folds. The sound of the rectangle will out quietly, will blacken down the perimeter, push out, rise up [26]

These sentences will cluster as they break; they will grain the substrate with cover while dissolving the substrate with void. They will cluster and break, slope and cluster, slope and void, and will be a forming-devolving shape inside the chapter [32]

These sentences will combine at dawn, intersecting sightlessly, and will not always say what they mean but will be breathing [98]

These sentences will constellate the gears that alter your movements on weather; they will foment tiny gears of speech, clicking, turning, moating, and will be like wind blowing thought back onto itself, behind itself so that thought moves by leaning forward [18]

These sentences will constellate the territories of the poem and will be the unraveling of the middle interior sky, too early arriving to the membranous sky, and will thin to the exterior [118]

These sentences will cover the horizon from end to end as a kind of castellation of grains and threads and portals; these portals will constitute the loop inside the map and will give the map levity [12]

These sentences will dome the thought; they will make complex gestures and grain on a curve. They will set memories in overlapping modes of slope and cover, making hollows [24]

These sentences will dome their alliances and make a castellation through a succession of awns [42]

These sentences will double as they blacken and will make something flying be something anchored and something swooping be the inverse of something housing; and will still be a house [26]

These sentences will draw inward when they arrive at the diaphanous chapter, the how-to-build, how-to-bridge chapter, and will be a blackened scree inside the luminous hidden within a proposition of houses [112]

These sentences will dream in a thinning-leaning across the substrate; they will loop the unknown and un-finish it [22]

These sentences will dream themselves into a figuration of planets and satellites, looking to set value to vari-ables beyond the science of the plain: the feeling of the unknown beside you [92]

These sentences will drop the nominative as a translation of sticks, geometrically, and will pull the number to the letter, will pour texture on the plain and crust the chapter [98]

These sentences will edge the void, will edge the plain and edge the towering structure; they will grain and blacken where they house and swoop where they fail [28]

These sentences will electrify the plain with black gathering; they will be blackened and will rise and cleave, magnetically, in an intake of housing [28]

These sentences will emerge as sites built haphazardly upon a fog ground and will be winded [94]

These sentences will enact a small striation of fields, a thinning of surfaces [14]

These sentences will erase half of what they say and will blight. They will make an unraveling that will void at the edges and will be an inland going from blight to grain; they will grain [50]

These sentences will filament the connection between phrases; will gasp the void and comma. They will detail the thinning of structures and will be the thinning itself [114]

These sentences will flood the plain in a repetition of walls and living; they will bend through scaffolds and flatten as they rise and be a floor for sky [4]

These sentences will flute and fold where the chapter crusts with questions [8]

These sentences will form a canopy of slow-moving sites and will cluster after fog and open after quiet [80]

These sentences will form a sanctuary for refusal; they will fan out, they will awn and cleave a new scaffold [58]

These sentences will funnel the plain in a bout of weather between the boundary and the front; they will rotate above and grain below. They will over and back above, will grain and blacken below. They will make an underground for your breathing, a repeating of devoted enclosure [58]

These sentences will gather all the pauses into a flowing assembly, into a speech that is only the comma, and will hold time as it distills and blackens in equation [20]

These sentences will gesture morning in the talking structure; they will be the blackening of the plain and the crowding of the light, be erased by light, without wind [112]

These sentences will glow where they blacken and be a figuration of edge to void to slope to void and will cleave as an outpost [78]

These sentences will grain along the seam, will blacken the seam, will thread through the seam three times and three times will thread its unsaying [36]

These sentences will grow grasses as the chapter ends and these grasses will signal the plain but also cut the substrate. Yet, the structure will hold. These will be the gaps [44]

These sentences will grow the field against the substrate in a theory of hills and they will spire [4]

These sentences will have a prop for resting at their centers, a pause in their unfolding for the subject, a bridge for wonder. They will thin where they close and will parse the luminous [82]

These sentences will have climbed the helical field, been a scaffolding of filaments, elaborations on thinning in thinning air, airless atmosphere—all air [74]

These sentences will have erupted from the plain, among the ruins of several burnt-out bunkers, your silo farm, and they will grain from the earth, each with a bending horizon and one vector pointing to space. They will cluster and contort [14]

These sentences will have moved vertically up the wall and made the floor the grain and made the grain a kind of seismic modulate unfolding [16]

These sentences will have performed the dreams of sentences upon arrival [18]

These sentences will have repeated while entrenching and will have glowed while rolling and will have been the systematic treatment of magnitude, being the underdoings of the colon, the em dash, the room behind the side of [108]

These sentences will have retreated into the territory long before we arrive, so what they say will be too quiet and too cold to hear; they will sit between two impossible walls in our dream of the journey, voiding against the rectangle [102]

These sentences will have shelter [120]

These sentences will have vectors that enter where they edge and will go to hollows, will curve to void and cleave to edge; they will funnel fourteen times and void [68]

These sentences will hive and grain within an enfoldment; they will dream where they cleave and void against blight, rising out of the plain. They will spire and roll and open. They will slope and hum and filament the slow-going [86]

These sentences will house the hidden beyond the curve and will thin at their saying [26]

These sentences will keep their core lit throughout the event of this writing and will attempt to grow a floor out of an introduction then build an essay under the floor and have math be the ghosts [110]

These sentences will lattice the substrate into composites of light and wire; they will fog the monument in a curving; they will fog the ground in memory. They will void the key [90]

These sentences will line the plain in modules for listening; they will hold and wait and lean in an absence of weather; they will be the calmative for the field [40]

These sentences will make a small equation against three thin lines cutting at the diagonal and will go quiet at the edge [54]

These sentences will make a tight, enclosing harmonics where the linking phrases turn and gasp in miniature and will lean in muted light [40]

These sentences will model a scale of the exhaustion of the erased [92]

These sentences will move around an extending gasping, a series of openings in the field; they will pour texture as an intervening and will awn in the leaves, the chapter growing dark where they gather [44]

These sentences will move forward in a kind of corridor duration and will shape the stringing of something linear and climbing—calling out a gull flying over water—to something triangular and graining—calling out water in water; and they will blacken at the hinge and double the ground [34]

These sentences will move invisibly through their not-knowing [114]

These sentences will move through other sentences in some accord of gravity and rotation; they will detour at the escapements then tunnel out to void [14]

These sentences will narrow in an out-and-through and leave behind a blackening that is also a map: they will tendril and grain and rise with nominative force. They will close the caption [86]

These sentences will open at a slope in a cartography of grain and wire; something will be said that is not exactly complete and it will curve, will up, will be a monument for this page [30]

These sentences will open the chapter on the electromagnetic and will be the reeling measure, the leaning, narrowing measure that detects the underground [16]

These sentences will reflect many places sitting in the same place; they will rise with breathing and will fold at the apex [110]

These sentences will river around silence and will out and vanish [62]

These sentences will round and hold as they lean; they will void in their interior but will hold. They will cleave the last refrain and go quiet; they will open and blacken [64]

These sentences will round then slope then lapse; they will void then thin then fail. They will cluster at the edge and open. They will round at the edge and void [64]

These sentences will seam the thinning [22]

These sentences will shade the block; they will form the substrate and shade. They will find their peaks and flutter in the corner. They will shade and flutter [10]

These sentences will shoal in their linearity; they will march to void and march to blacken. They will edge and thicken and double the horizon. They will blacken [6]

These sentences will signal the closing of the figurations, the soon-to-be end of planning, the growing short of breathing [114]

These sentences will slope in their unfolding and will consent to an overlapping, to a piling on of, and will float the environment to void and will blacken it to mountain [32]

These sentences will sonar the sea while the land mosses; they will blur where they blacken and will rise interiorly. They will out and reel and over with conduction; they will rise and thin and out [30]

These sentences will strain the curve against the graining, the diagonal against the curve, and will burn equidistant to what unfolds. They will form a scaffold of ascending and descending clauses and will know space [10]

These sentences will take place in three modes simultaneously; they will shade in the measure of the space that holds them and curve to laddering, making a lattice but only up to void. They will out where they void and return where they edge and will forget themselves [106]

These sentences will take the line of the smear without smearing and will fall below the fault of the page; they will grain and cluster independent and complete of the horizon [74]

These sentences will tend the slow cleaving of the field; they will over and up, they will grain and cluster, they will ripple at the edge. They will void [22]

These sentences will thin the plain and scratch the void then cluster into undergrounds, a thinning of undergrounds; they will edge the void and blacken where they house [16]

These sentences will turn fog into gaps and will allow the page to become a turning; something will turn that also will out and back quietly. The outside will glow from inside, becoming a window [114]

These sentences will void at the plain four times, wash out the ground twice, stutter twice, elongate; they will prolong the horizon [6]

These sentences will void, giving the filament the greater voice, the one straining ladder, the cluster falling into the open; there will be gasps and graining here and a rolling out and back that ripples the paragraph [24]

These sentences will wind tightly around who we are and how we live and will grow habitations as they wonder; they will cleave from the ground in enclosures of grief and will knoll [46]

These sentences will work the ground of the dreaming chapter into a commotion of waking: the ground waking inside the dream, the chapter waking inside a moving torque of hills [104]

These sites will be your monuments in cloud-heavy paragraphs; they will blacken and be your underground. They will curve and thin and will awn after closing; they will fail in twilight [84]

These thinning structures will be blowing in high winds for as long as this chapter exists, which will be al-
ways; they will tendril in loose piles and be like portals through the substrate. They will rise as they thin
[60]

These will be events returning [88]

These will be sentences that climb and blacken after fog, that fog out with wanting. They will roll tightly
against the substrate then will bellow [76]

These will be sentences upon which is reflected something unseen seeing. They will foment where they
empty, go quiet where they flood, be a staggering response to something missing, be a hull, a curve [56]

These will be the inhabitable sentences [114]

These will be the sky written on and the sky extending to the ground; these will blur their borders, they will
lean and darken and partition the ground from itself. These will be weather [88]

These will be those tiny sentences that come at the end of some meandering thought, stuttering between
conclusion and silence [102]

These will cleave in tiny gasps of living, one on top of another; they will run the circle of the page and will
leave the circle to the void; they will dome and out quietly [38]

These will climb the substrate: they will roll. They will roll and go quiet. They will roll, a line burning into the
surface. They will over backward and will over the start and over the interruption; they will roll and square
the void [10]

These will crust a scaffold, will chapter the site as it striates, and will write the unwritten without pause. They
will encumber to void [12]

These will distill the question about the weather—"Is it fine?" "Are you fine today?" They will flute and
silo [40]

These will emerge from grain: they will out and open. They will over and back and open. They will edge and
cross and grain [2]

These will exist without walls but will have domes then fog [84]

These will flutter and spire and go dark with grain [28]

These will form an assembly of poles and pour texture through the nominative [34]

These will grain into a geometry of support, the history of something burrowing [8]

These will hang in staggered formation for what you're saying and will corner and roll; they will be the glowing chapters and will show the ley lines beneath the weather report [72]

These will have ended in a spire, in reach of elsewhere, the other side of bringing things in to know them; they will have wanted to preserve the gasps as tiny communities but will have been thought mostly to void, to believe upward, and will have finished at the filament [58]

These will have gone up, a thin line, and bent, just going right and bending then reaching up: growing something, will grow a question an aside, an aside to the question, some stutter, and a period at the top [14]

These will hive; they will bellow [48]

These will name little waters that comma, that lean [72]

These will out and over and grain and through and around; they will shade and climb the substrate and spire. They will shade and cut the plain, leave a ladder [38]

These will set something at the back of something and make it larger; what is smallest will be at the forefront but also below. These will bend, will contort. They will grain [24]

These will shoal and form a chamber just outside the dream; they will assume the energy of a dispersing hive and will blight the history [48]

These will slope from trying [68]

They will be made of wind and will gasp, will allow gasps to become walls then will bellow and fray [52]

They will be wall-less, curved enclosures for voice, clauses for loss, graining for the collective; they will open and climb and swoop diaphanously [84]

They will build upon a notion of the half-silo, the floorless outdoors [54]

They will cleave as they crust and round as they flood the plain; they will over and shade then wire and cleave; they will glow beneath the smear [32]

They will erupt from the surface in an alternative mode of pointing and will stand variously and voidly under impulses to curve and flute; they will curve and flute without history [8]

They will have speed, and this will be what pleases, what funnels the valley to void; they will have gasps where they bridge and will figment [94]

They will have the one thing leaning and the other thing sloping and will divide the plain just below the densest language and will launch the language of the grain [4]

They will make a system out of graining and will build on the break; they will sit, they will stand then void. They will thin then crust then glow; they will elapse. They will grain an underground, a bright hollow [82]

They will not know space [10]

They will out quietly in a thin single line of fanning, they will turn, they will counter; they will turn and land and lift off and turn within the meditation, and will blacken gasps into the page [46]

They will roll out of light into light [62]

They will send out fraying signals, will lean away from the hull and into the wing [52]

They will set the world of the text in motion, diverting at the escapement, turning to void, and will make small bodies of sayings that will click and moat [18]

They will sonar the erased [56]

They will spire threaded towers, and behind them hives will rise belonging to language, but not these sentences of any language and not this language in particular [20]

They will stack and out and hinge. These sentences will hold; they will slope and edge and double. They will fail at the thinning. They will double in the center [80]

This chapter will ache a massive threading and glow; it will stand at the end of all chapters and reclaim its geometries. It will weather and glow in an overlay of forms and will buckle where it cleaves [76]

This chapter will be about laughter and a doming light; there will be gasps and a set of ascending enclosures, everything moving up on a slope, curving as it rolls out [116]

This chapter will be the dark glowing fog over the substrate, the void opening to cleave; it will edge the unwritten into a shape of something wrote and will be read from graining, be a thinning [82]

This chapter will be the site of all the commas fleeing [102]

This chapter will be the weather report on full blast, your opening paragraph moaning: so much light [108]

This chapter will comprise 465 passages without words; and there will be a gray happening [98]

This chapter will have exploded from its interior shading and will enumerate with force, in a force of clouds [88]

This chapter will open the face of the book, revealing a series of active escapements, linking place to place. These will steady the dissolving map, be an intricacy of dome, be a slope cut along an edge [38]

This chapter will represent a gap in the paragraph, a time between words, and will shade loudly the evacuated and be a black luminous, slow-going forward [92]

This chapter will self-intersect as well as any poem or weather map; it will blacken as it figures: be a thinning, be dark. And will chart a history of wander [118]

This chapter will slide into your math diaphanously and will make a memoir of your space problem: the concentric to the grain upon the slope to the stacked. It will blacken with enfoldment [80]

This chapter will write itself in intervals of fog and twilight; it will filament the curve and be a chronicle. It will curve and close then curve and fog and will glow where it blackens. It will grain and blacken and void [90]

ACKNOWLEDGMENTS

I began this series of drawings in Seattle in spring 2016 and continued through the fall of that same year. Despite the intervening publication of *One Long Black Sentence* in 2020, this is the work that directly follows *Prose Architectures*, in terms of the evolution of my mark-making and my continued devotion to the entwinement of drawing and writing. *Plans for Sentences* were made using the TWSBI Diamond 580AL fountain pen with (at turns) F, M, and B nibs in sepia ink on 11 × 14-inch mixed media paper. The series comprises 137 drawings, of which sixty are presented here.

In fall 2018, while at an artist residency at Denniston Hill, I began writing the text for this book. For a long time, I hadn't wanted legible, narrative language anywhere near my drawings. I felt that no matter how I arranged them, one or the other (i.e., the text or the drawing) would fall into the category of illustration. I wasn't interested in that dynamic until I was. At the same time, I started to wonder: What would future sentences look like and what would they do in a present that precedes their use or, at least, precedes the places to which they point? These are descriptions for future sentences, however the *plans* for those sentences (i.e., their actual futures) are still the drawings.

Thank you to Jessica Rankin and the other members of the board at Denniston Hill for providing a beautiful and productive space to work; to Maxwell Mutanda, architect and artist, also in residence, for his bright, sweet presence and cohabitation; and to the musician Rosali for her song "If I Was Your Heart," which I listened to on endless repeat.

Plans for Sentences #59 was published as *Territories of the Poem* by *Brooklyn Rail* in a special section edited by Ann Lauterbach. Thank you, Ann. *Plans for Sentences #52* was previously published online as *Plans for Sentences #88* in *e-flux journal* #92.

And deepest thanks to my editor, Heidi Broadhead, who is both a precise and expansive reader.

*

This book is dedicated to Danielle Vogel. I would not have had the language or emotion to write this book were it not for this past decade of life with you. Thank you, my love.